こどものためのピアノ曲集

ぬいぐるみのゆめ

小森昭宏　作曲

The piano pieces for CHILDREN for small hands

DREAM OF MY CUDDLY BEAR

composed by Akihiro Komori

edition KAWAI

皆様へのお願い

楽譜や歌詞・音楽書などの出版物を権利者に無断で複製（コピー）することは、著作権の侵害（私的利用など特別な場合を除く）にあたり、著作権法により罰せられます。また、出版物からの不法なコピーが行われますと、出版社は正常な出版活動が困難となり、ついには皆様方が必要とされるものも出版できなくなります。

音楽出版社と日本音楽著作権協会（JASRAC）は、著作者の権利を守り、なおいっそう優れた作品の出版普及に全力をあげて努力してまいります。どうか不法コピーの防止に、皆様方のご協力をお願い申しあげます。

カワイ出版
一般社団法人　日本音楽著作権協会

はじめに

　どんなにやさしく弾ける曲でも、音楽には、なにかの表現・表情がなくてはいけません。作曲家は、聴いている人に何かを感じてもらいたくて曲を書いています。

　私も小さい時からピアノを習いましたが、あとになってから、初めの頃に弾いていた曲には、運指の訓練を目的にしたものが多く、子供の興味をひくような曲は、あまりなかったように思います。

　運指も大事ですが、感情・感覚を育てることのほうが、もっともっと大切です。

　大脳の生理から考えても、運指は言わば運動神経の領域ですが、音楽には、もっと沢山の、情緒や感情の部分をつかさどる、脳神経が関係しています。その、情緒や感情を発達させるような曲というものがあるはずです。

　運指の訓練を目的にした、何の表現も必要としない曲は、この曲集にはありません。

　聴いている人の心に響くもの、それが音楽です。こどものための、やさしい曲にも「聴いている人の心にうったえる何かがなくてはいけない。」と思いますし、また「豊かな感性を持つ人に育ってもらえるように。」との願いをこめて、この曲集を書きました。

1995年8月

小 森 昭 宏

PREFACE

Every music must have a certain expression of its own however easy it is to play. Composers write a piece because they want the listeners to feel something.
I began to learn playing the piano when I was a very young child, as is often the case, and I noticed after years that there were few pieces of real interest to children that attract excitement among those for beginners but most of all were only meant to be for finger training.
Finger training might be important, I admit, but it surely is much more important to develop one's feeling or sense for music.
In view of cerebric physiology, fingering is naturally classified in the field of what is called motor nerve. But music has a much closer relation to cranial nerve which controls emotion and feelings of human beings. There must be a certain kind of pieces that help one develop one's emotion and feelings.
Never did I includ in this collection such pieces without any expression as are intended only for finger training.
To reach the heart of every listener — that is what music is to be. I believe any music must have something to appeal to the heart of listeners even if it is easy enough for children to play. I wrote every one of those pieces for this collection in the hope that dear learners should grow up to be highly sensitive to music.

Akihiro Komori

August 1995

も く じ / CONTENTS

		演奏時間	Page
1.	矢車草のワルツ WALTZ FOR BLUEBOTTLE	（約1分40秒）	6
2.	江戸の夕暮れ TWILIGHT EVENING IN EDO	（約2分00秒）	8
3.	すみれが好きなロバの話 TALE OF A DONKEY WHO LOVES VIOLETS	（約1分46秒）	10
4.	鳩のお母さんに聞いたお話 THE STORY I HEARD FROM MOTHER PIGEON	（約1分36秒）	12
5.	こおろぎの好きなワルツ WALTZ OF THE CRICKET'S FAVORITE	（約2分05秒）	14
6.	ジェーンのワルツ JANE'S WALTZ	（約1分43秒）	18
7.	王子さまは馬にのって SOMEDAY MY PRINCE WILL COME ON A HORSE	（約2分30秒）	20
8.	友達と けんかしちゃった I'VE HAD A PETTY QUARREL WITH A FRIEND	（約1分38秒）	22
9.	まいごになった メダカ STRAY MEDAKA	（約2分40秒）	24
10.	昔、中国のお姫様が見た夢 DREAM THAT THE CHINESE PRINCESS HAD A LONG LONG TIME AGO	（約2分14秒）	26
11.	バラが好きな アルマジロの話 TALE OF AN ARMADILLO WHO LOVES ROSES	（約1分47秒）	28

		演奏時間	Page

12. サンバ・サボテン
SAMBA CACTUS ………… (約1分18秒) ………… 30

13. 昔、砂漠の地下にあった宮殿
PALACE OF A DISTANT PAST UNDER THE DESERT ………… (約1分55秒) ………… 32

14. ぬいぐるみが見た夢
DREAM OF MY CUDDLY BEAR ………… (約2分02秒) ………… 34

15. スペースシャトルの朝
MORNING IN THE SPACE SHUTTLE ………… (約2分20秒) ………… 36

16. 火星人の好きな行進曲
MARCH OF THE MARTIANS' FAVORITE ………… (約2分05秒) ………… 38

17. ロバさんの荷物はこび
LOADED DONKEY ………… (約2分30秒) ………… 41

18. かざぐるまの たより
LETTER FROM THE WINDMILL ………… (約1分55秒) ………… 44

19. サンフランシスコの おみやげ
SOUVENIR FROM SAN FRANCISCO ………… (約1分46秒) ………… 48

20. カメさんのブギ
TURTLE'S BOOGIE ………… (約1分52秒) ………… 50

21. 透明人間
INVISIBLE MAN ………… (約2分11秒) ………… 52

22. ニューヨークへ行こう
LET'S GO TO NEW YORK ………… (約1分25秒) ………… 54

23. 遠い森のむこうのお話
TALE OF THE FOREST IN THE FAR DISTANCE ………… (約2分45秒) ………… 56

24. 宇宙遊泳
SPACEWALK ………… (約2分32秒) ………… 58

25. 壬生狂言のテーマによるパラフレーズ
PARAPHRASE ON THE THEME FROM "MIBU KYOGEN" ………… (約3分30秒) ………… 60

1. 矢車草のワルツ
WALTZ FOR BLUEBOTTLE

音を少なくしましたが、かわいらしさ、やさしさ、などの表情は充分出せるはずです。
Codaの部分は *accel.* して、*f* で盛り上げてください。

Though the written notes are minimum, they must be enough to express the loveliness and tenderness of bluebottle.
In coda, put *accel.* and reach the climax in *f*.

小森昭宏　作曲
Akihiro Komori

2. 江戸の夕暮れ
TWILIGHT EVENING IN EDO

日本情緒の曲です。
5小節目からのメロディ四小節は、「神田ばやし」のなかの一節です。
右手は笛のつもりで弾いてください。夕暮れの、落ち着いた江戸情緒が出れば良いと思います。

Edo is the old name of Tokyo, and here is presented the Japanese traditional emotion.
A phrase from "Kanda-bayashi," one of the famous Japanese festival songs, is quoted in the melody over the 4 bars beginning from the 5th bar.
Play your left hand like a Japanese fue, a Japanese traditional instrument that resembles the flute.
My intention is a quiet feeling of Edo in the twilight.

小森昭宏　作曲
Akihiro Komori

©Copyright 1996 by edition KAWAI, Tokyo, Japan.
International Copyright Secured, All Rights Reserved.

3. すみれが好きなロバの話
TALE OF A DONKEY WHO LOVES VIOLETS

低音部に十度ができて、こどもの曲であっても、こどもの演奏であっても、豊かな響きがするように作りました。**Moderato**のところは、ロバさんが、すみれの花にうっとりしているところです。やさしい気持ちで弾いてください。

The effect of the 10th interval in the bass makes the piece sound rich even though it is written for children to be performed by children.
The section of Moderato is the scene that the donkey is fascinated by the flowers of violet. Play as gently.

小森昭宏 作曲
Akihiro Komori

©Copyright 1996 by edition KAWAI, Tokyo, Japan.
International Copyright Secured, All Rights Reserved.

4. 鳩のお母さんに聞いたお話
THE STORY I HEARD FROM MOTHER PIGEON

鳩とお話しているような、優しい気持ちで弾いてください。
手の指の形をあまり動かさないで弾けるように、考えました。

Play as gently as if you were talking to pigeons.
I tried to make fingering as simple as possible.

小森昭宏　作曲
Akihiro Komori

©Copyright 1996 by edition KAWAI, Tokyo, Japan.
International Copyright Secured, All Rights Reserved.

5. こおろぎの好きなワルツ
WALTZ OF THE CRICKET'S FAVORITE

3拍子ですが、1・2・3、と等間隔に機械的に拍子を考えずに、すこしのテンポのゆれがあったほうが表情が出ると思います。そのためもあって、左手は、1・2拍しか拍子をきざんでいません。
頭の中で拍子をこしらえてください。

This is a triple-time piece. Do not make the beat equal and automatic "1, 2, 3," but make it so flexible and free as to add to your rich expression, Taking it into account, I only wrote the first two beats for the left hand.
Create the third beat in your own mind.

小森昭宏　作曲
Akihiro Komori

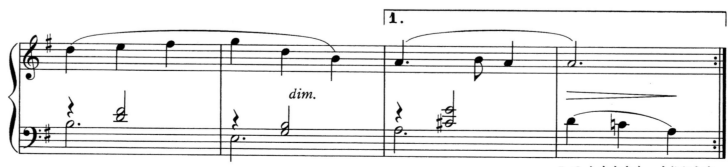

※ *D. C.* したときも、くりかえす。
Repeat again after *D. C.*

©Copyright 1996 by edition KAWAI, Tokyo, Japan.
International Copyright Secured, All Rights Reserved.

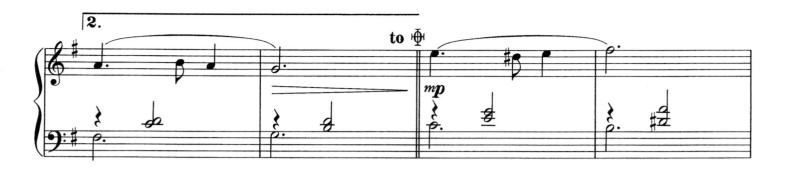

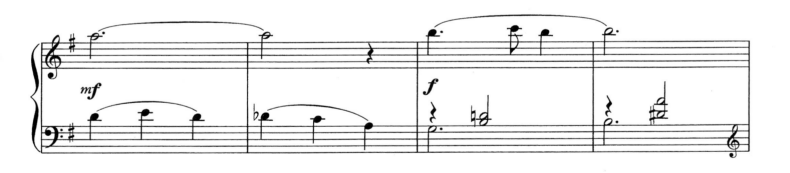

6. ジェーンのワルツ
JANE'S WALTZ

この曲は、ある演劇公演のために書いたもので、おばあさんになったジェーンが、夢の中で昔好きだった人と踊る場面の曲です。
そのときは、オルゴールで演奏しましたが、ピアノで弾く時も、すこしその事を考えに入れて弾くと、きれいに弾けるかもしれません。
This piece was originally written for a certain drama performance, accompanying the scene that Jane, an old woman, dances in her dream with somebody she used to love when she was young.
At that time in the live performance, it was played by a music box, and now you play it on the piano. Just think of the sound of a music box and you would surely be the better performer.

©Copyright 1996 by edition KAWAI, Tokyo, Japan.
International Copyright Secured, All Rights Reserved.

7. 王子さまは 馬にのって
SOMEDAY MY PRINCE WILL COME ON A HORSE

左手は馬の足音のつもりで、正確にリズムをきざみましょう。
右手は、表情豊かに、感情をこめて弾きましょう。
あなたが男なら王子様になったつもりで、女ならお姫様になったつもりで。

The left hand should beat the rhythm accurately, supposing it to be the footsteps of a horse.
Play the right hand so expressively and emotionally.
Imagine yourself to be a prince if you are a boy, or a princess if you are a girl.

小森昭宏 作曲
Akihiro Komori

©Copyright 1996 by edition KAWAI, Tokyo, Japan.
International Copyright Secured, All Rights Reserved.

8. 友達と けんかしちゃった
I'VE HAD A PETTY QUARREL WITH A FRIEND

友達とけんかして、ちょっと悲しくなりますが、どちらがあやまったのでしょうか、またもとのように仲良くなりました。

He was sad because he had a petty quarrel with his friend, but soon again they made it up with each other. Which one do you think apologized?

小森昭宏　作曲
Akihiro Komori

©Copyright 1996 by edition KAWAI, Tokyo, Japan.
International Copyright Secured, All Rights Reserved.

9. まいごになった メダカ
STRAY MEDAKA

はじめは、元気にメダカが泳いでいますが、2番カッコのあたりから、まいごになったメダカはすこし寂しくなります。
でも、すぐに元気をとりもどしてお友達をさがしにいきます。かわいいですね。

In the beginning a stray medaka is sailing cheerfully, but it comes to feel lonely around at the 2.mark.
But then again it soon regained its spirits and went sailing to look for its friends, Isn't it lovely？

小森昭宏 作曲
Akihiro Komori

©Copyright 1996 by edition KAWAI, Tokyo, Japan.
International Copyright Secured, All Rights Reserved.

10. 昔、中国のお姫様が見た夢
DREAM THAT THE CHINESE PRINCESS HAD A LONG LONG TIME AGO

昔の中国のお姫様はどんな生活をしていたのでしょう。本や博物館・歴史館等で調べてみるのも良いでしょう。
左手は簡単なくりかえしですが、右手のメロディを歌わせてください。
やさしい気持ちで、お姫様がどんな夢を見たのか、想像しながら弾いてください。

What do you think was the life of the ancient Chinese Princess like ? You can find it out in books or at a museum or a history museum.
Sing the melody on your right hand in contrast to the simple repetition on your left hand.
Imagine how the dream went on that the princess had, and play it with a soft heart.

小森昭宏　作曲
Akihiro Komori

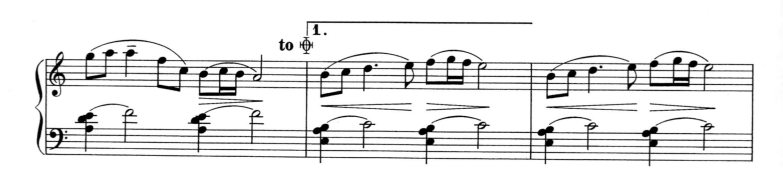

©Copyright 1996 by edition KAWAI, Tokyo, Japan.
International Copyright Secured, All Rights Reserved.

11. バラが好きなアルマジロの話
TALE OF AN ARMADILLO WHO LOVES ROSES

ときどき臨時記号がついて、転調しますが、指の形はあまり動かさずに済むようにしてあります。
やさしく語りかけるように弾いてください。

Here appear some accidentals and the piece modulates at times, but you can make it in simple fingering.
Play so gently as if you were talking to someone.

小森昭宏　作曲
Akihiro Komori

©Copyright 1996 by edition KAWAI, Tokyo, Japan.
International Copyright Secured, All Rights Reserved.

12. サンバ・サボテン
SAMBA CACTUS

南米音楽のリズムの一つである、サンバです。16ビートともいわれるこのリズムは、今聴くポピュラー音楽だけでなく、ほとんどの音楽に少なからず影響を与えているのが、この南米音楽だと言えるでしょう。
テレビやラジオ、CDでサンバ・リズムの音楽を聴いて、リズム感を身につけましょう。

This rhythm is called samba, or 16 beat, originating in the South American music. It is the South American music that has had quite an influence upon not only today's popular music but almost all kinds of music.
Listen to the music of samba rhythm on TV, radio, and CDs, and get that sense of rhythm.

小森昭宏 作曲
Akihiro Komori

©Copyright 1996 by edition KAWAI, Tokyo, Japan.
International Copyright Secured, All Rights Reserved.

13. 昔、砂漠の地下にあった宮殿
PALACE OF A DISTANT PAST UNDER THE DESERT

大きな宮殿を頭の中に思い浮かべてください。
ゆっくりな曲で、うごきが多くなく、やさしく弾ける曲ですが、小さいこどもでも、豊かな響きが
出せるように、工夫しました。

Imagine a grand palace in your mind.
This is a slow piece with little motion, and is easy to play in a sense. I just tried to make it simple so that you can create a good and rich sound even if you are a very young child.

14. ぬいぐるみが見た夢
DREAM OF MY CUDDLY BEAR

子守歌です。
歌って聴かせるつもりで弾きましょう。
低音部に十度ができて、豊かな響きがするように作ってあります。
This is a lullaby.
You are supposed to sing it for someone.
The 10th interval made by a bass note is intended for a grand and rich sound.

小森昭宏 作曲
Akihiro Komori

©Copyright 1996 by edition KAWAI, Tokyo, Japan.
International Copyright Secured, All Rights Reserved.

15. スペースシャトルの朝
MORNING IN THE SPACE SHUTTLE

左手は、単純な形のくりかえしですが、一小節の間で、その調にない和音が重なって出てきます。
たとえば、一番始めの小節は、ヘ長調と変ホ長調ですが、ヘ長調にない、Esの和音を組み合わせる事で、なにか地上ではない、現実と掛け離れた状態を表現しようとしてみました。

The left hand plays a simple repetition of simple patterns, but notice that there appear some unfamiliar chords within a bar which do not belong to the original key.

The first bar, for example, is written in F major and there appears a chord of Es major. I intended this combination to express something quite alien to the reality that would never exist on the earth.

小森昭宏 作曲
Akihiro Komori

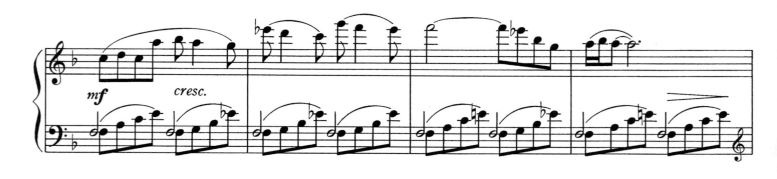

©Copyright 1996 by edition KAWAI, Tokyo, Japan.
International Copyright Secured, All Rights Reserved.

16. 火星人の好きな行進曲
MARCH OF THE MARTIANS' FAVORITE

マーチです。左手の1拍目と3拍目はアクセントをつけてください。
火星人に会ったことはありませんが、人間に似ていたらこの曲を好きになってくれるかもしれません。
火星にとどくように、元気に弾いてください。
This is a march. Put an accent on the first and the third beat on your left hand.
Martians might like this piece if they have something in common with us, though I have never met them.
Play vigorously so that it would reach the Mars.

小森昭宏　作曲
Akihiro Komori

Moderato ♩=120 くらい

©Copyright 1996 by edition KAWAI, Tokyo, Japan.
International Copyright Secured, All Rights Reserved.

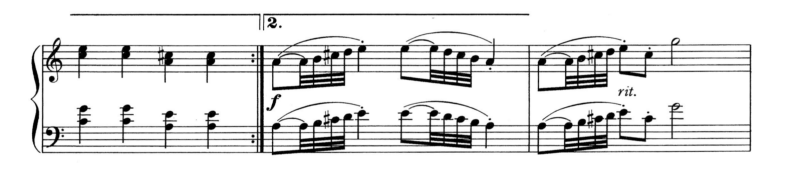

17. ロバさんの 荷物はこび
LOADED DONKEY

ロバさんが、重い荷物を運んでいます。左手の1・2・3・4拍の頭には、アクセントをつけてください。
17小節目から四小節間はすこしくたびれた感じで、*rit.* があったほうが良いでしょう。
最後はうんとがんばって、やれやれと終わってください。

The donkey is loaded with a heavy load. Put an accent on every beat of 1,2,3, and 4 on your left hand.
During the 4 bars from the 17th to 20th, please do not forget to play with *rit.* and that with a little tired feeling.
In the final section, you have to exert all your powers and you can give a sigh of relief in the end.

小森昭宏　作曲
Akihiro Komori

©Copyright 1996 by edition KAWAI, Tokyo, Japan.
International Copyright Secured, All Rights Reserved.

18. かざぐるまの たより
LETTER FROM THE WINDMILL

右手は16分音符の同じ形が続きますが、ほとんど指の形を変えずに、しかも指をかえさずに弾けますので、見た目よりずっとやさしい曲です。
流れるように、*dim. cresc.* ƒ, ₚ, 等の記号に気をつけて、優しい気持ちで弾いてください。

Sequent patterns of sixteenth notes are to be played by your right hand. But there is almost no need to make changes in your finger position, and that you do not even need to cross your fingers. So this is a much easier piece to play than it seems.
Just pay attention to those articulation marks such as *dim.*, *cresc.*, ƒ, ₚ, etc. and play gently.

小森昭宏　作曲
Akihiro Komori

©Copyright 1996 by edition KAWAI, Tokyo, Japan.
International Copyright Secured, All Rights Reserved.

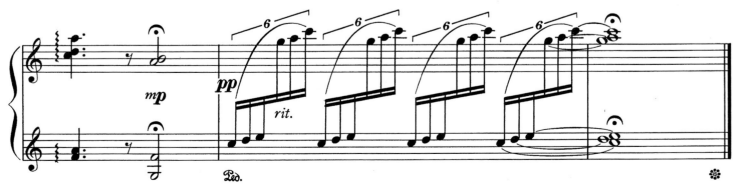

19. サンフランシスコの おみやげ
SOUVENIR FROM SAN FRANCISCO

スイング・ジャズです。音楽にはいろいろな種類があります。いろいろな音楽はそれぞれに影響しあって発展してきました。
ジャズもそうです。基本的なジャズの弾き方のひとつを覚えましょう。

This is a swing jazz. There are many various kinds in music. Influenced by one another, they all have developed in their own way.
So is jazz. Here you can learn one of the basic performances in jazz.

小森昭宏　作曲
Akihiro Komori

©Copyright 1996 by edition KAWAI, Tokyo, Japan.
International Copyright Secured, All Rights Reserved.

20. カメさんのブギ
TURTLE'S BOOGIE

ジャズのなかの一つの形式に、ブルースというのがあります。ブギウギもブルースの中の一つで、12小節で一区切りになっているのが特徴で、和音の進行もほとんど決まっています。
何人かの演奏家が集まって、たとえば「F調でブルースをやろう」と決まれば、何時間でも代わりあって即興演奏が続けられるという、とても便利なものです。

Boogie-woogie is a kind of blues which is a form categorized in jazz. It is characterized by the unit of 12 bars with the customary chord progression.
So it is very convenient when it comes to unexpected improvisation among some musicians, because all they have to do is to decide the key, for example, "Let's make it in F major," and they can keep on and on playing blues even for hours by turns.

小森昭宏　作曲
Akihiro Komori

©Copyright 1996 by edition KAWAI, Tokyo, Japan.
International Copyright Secured, All Rights Reserved.

21. 透明人間
INVISIBLE MAN

「本当は、私は見えません！」とか言ってステージに出てくると面白いかもしれません。
透明なレインコートなんか着ると、もっと良いかもしれません。
ちょっと気味が悪いけれど、みんなが喜んでくれるのではないでしょうか。
楽譜に書いてあるように、聴いている人達に向いて「ハーッ！」と言うと、きっとみんな、大笑いしますよ。

It might be entertaining if you appeared on the stage saying something like "Actually, I am supposed to be invisible !"
Or it might be much better if you were dressed in a transparent raincoat.
You might feel a little uncomfortable, but I am sure the audience should be pleased to see you and your performance.
As is written on the music, if you say "Ha !" to the audience, they would roar with laughter.

小森昭宏 作曲
Akihiro Komori

©Copyright 1996 by edition KAWAI, Tokyo, Japan.
International Copyright Secured, All Rights Reserved.

※ 聴いている人達に向かって、茶目っ気たっぷりに無声音で「ハーッ！」と言う。
Mischievously say "Ha !" to the audience with a voiceless sound.

22. ニューヨークへ行こう
LET'S GO TO NEW YORK

スイング・ジャズです。
テレビやラジオ、CDで聴く、プロの演奏を参考にして、リズム感を身に付けるように心掛けましょう。
This is a swing jazz.
Try to learn a good sense of rhythm. It will be helpful to you to listen to those professional performances of jazz on TV, radio, or CDs.

小森昭宏 作曲
Akihiro Komori

©Copyright 1996 by edition KAWAI, Tokyo, Japan.
International Copyright Secured, All Rights Reserved.

23. 遠い森のむこうのお話
TALE OF THE FOREST IN THE FAR DISTANCE

低音に十度が出来て、豊かな響きがするように作ってあります。
右手は、メロディと、拍作りの両方をやらなければなりませんが、メロディを大きく豊かに歌うように
心掛けてください。

The 10th interval, made by an effective bass note, is intended to bring forth rich sound.
The right hand has to take part in both singing the melody and making the beat. Always be conscious of the rich and grand expression of melody and sing it.

小森昭宏 作曲
Akihiro Komori

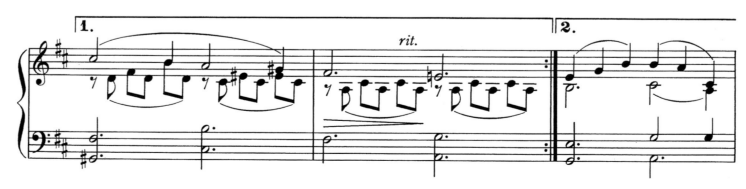

©Copyright 1996 by edition KAWAI, Tokyo, Japan.
International Copyright Secured, All Rights Reserved.

24. 宇宙遊泳
SPACEWALK

黒鍵のグリッサンドと、ペダルの組み合わせで、やさしいのですが、幅の広い、大きな表現ができるように作ってある曲です。
たっぷりと、宇宙の大きさと神秘を味わってください。
This is a combination of glissando on the black keys and pedalling. It must be easy enough for you to express a wide and grand expression.
I want you to enjoy the vast expanse and mystery of the space world to your heart's content.

小森昭宏　作曲
Akihiro Komori

25. 壬生狂言のテーマによるパラフレーズ
PARAPHRASE ON THE THEME FROM "MIBU KYOGEN"

京都の壬生寺で毎年行なわれる狂言で使われる、笛とドラの曲のフレーズを、一曲に仕立て上げてみました。
実際は、頭のピアノの右手の2小節のメロディを笛が繰り返し、ドラが、"がんでんでん"とリズムを作っていく、簡単なものなのですが、いろいろな場面にもそれでぴたりと雰囲気があってしまうという、不思議な魅力のある曲ですので、前から、このフレーズを使って、なにか作りたいなと思っておりました。

Kyogen is a Noh farce, a kind of Japanese traditional play. This piece is based on a phrase by fue and gong accompanying the traditional kyogen which is annually performed at the Mibu Temple in Kyoto.
The original phrase is a very simple one that consists of a repetition of the fue's melody, which is to be played by the right hand here in the first two bars, accompanied by the gong's "ding-dong-dong" rhythm. Strangely enough, that very simple repetition would suit any scenes and make atmosphere of its own as the scene demands. It was my longstanding plan to write something with that attractive phrase.

小森昭宏 作曲
Akihiro Komori

©Copyright 1996 by edition KAWAI, Tokyo, Japan.
International Copyright Secured, All Rights Reserved.

Allegro ♩=130 くらい

携帯サイトはこちら▶

出版情報&ショッピング　カワイ出版ONLINE　http://editionkawai.jp

こどものためのピアノ曲集
ぬいぐるみのゆめ

発行日● 1996 年 1 月 1 日　　第 1 刷発行	作　曲●小森昭宏
2025 年 4 月 1 日　　第 17 刷発行	発行所●カワイ出版（株式会社 全音楽譜出版社 カワイ出版部）
	〒 161-0034　　東京都新宿区上落合 2-13-3
	TEL.03-3227-6286　FAX.03-3227-6296
表紙装幀・イラスト●津田直美	楽譜浄書●ミュージックリード
翻訳●前嶋律子	写植●フォトタイプ潤
	印刷 / 製本●平河工業社

© 1996 by edition KAWAI. Assigned 2017 to Zen-On Music Co., Ltd.

　本書よりの転載はお断りします。
　　　　　　　　　　 落丁・乱丁本はお取り替え致します。
　　　　　　　　　　 本書のデザインや仕様は予告なく変更される場合がございます。

ISBN978-4-7609-0525-6